In the Footsteps of Explorers

Daniel Boone

Woodsman of Kentucky

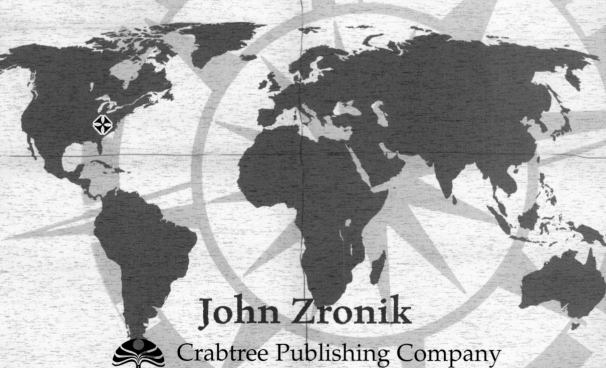

John Zronik

Crabtree Publishing Company

www.crabtreebooks.com

Crabtree Publishing Company

www.crabtreebooks.com

Coordinating editor: Ellen Rodger
Series editor: Carrie Gleason
Editors: Rachel Eagen, Adrianna Morganelli, L. Michelle Nielsen
Design and production coordinator: Rosie Gowsell
Cover design, layout, and production assistance: Samara Parent
Art direction: Rob MacGregor
Scanning technician: Arlene Arch-Wilson
Photo research: Allison Napier

Consultant: Daniel Boone Homestead

Photo Credits: Art Archive/Cherokee Indian Museum North Carolina/Mireille Vautier: p. 24 (top); Art Archive/Global Book Publishing: p. 30; Bettmann/Corbis: pp. 12-13, p. 27, p. 31; Raymond Gehman/Corbis: p. 11; The Granger Collection, New York: cover, p. 17, p. 20, pp. 28-29; Kimberly Deprey/istock International: p. 19 (top right); North Wind/Nancy Carter/North Wind Picture Archives: pp. 18-19; North Wind/North Wind Picture Archives: p. 5, p. 6, p. 7, p. 8, p. 9, p. 14, p. 15, p. 16, p. 18, p. 21, pp. 22-23, p. 23, p. 25, p. 26; Wisconsin Historical Society: p. 19 (top left); Other images from stock photo cd

Illustrations: Lauren Fast: p. 4, p. 31 (both)

Cartography: Jim Chernishenko: title page, p. 10

Cover: There are many myths about Daniel Boone. One myth is that Boone wore a coonskin hat. Boone's son, Nathan Boone, claimed that his father wore a beaver hat, yet some of the best known images of Boone show him wearing a coonskin hat.

Title page: Daniel Boone explored the Appalachian Mountains and trailblazed a road through the Cumberland Gap.

Sidebar icon: Boone encountered bears on his long hunting trips.

Crabtree Publishing Company

www.crabtreebooks.com   1-800-387-7650

Cataloging-in-Publication Data

Zronik, John Paul, 1972-
  Daniel Boone : woodsman of Kentucky / written by John Zronik.
    p. cm. -- (In the footsteps of explorers)
  Includes bibliographical references and index.
  ISBN-13: 978-0-7787-2428-5 (rlb)
  ISBN-10: 0-7787-2428-X (rlb)
  ISBN-13: 978-0-7787-2464-3 (pbk)
  ISBN-10: 0-7787-2464-6 (pbk)
 1. Boone, Daniel, 1734-1820--Juvenile literature. 2. Pioneers--Kentucky--Biography--Juvenile literature. 3. Explorers--Kentucky--Biography--Juvenile literature. 4. Frontier and pioneer life--Kentucky--Juvenile literature. 5. Kentucky--Biography--Juvenile literature. 6. Kentucky--Discovery and exploration--Juvenile literature. I. Title. II. Series.
  F454.B66Z76 2006
  976.9'02092--dc22   2005035759
                                                    LC

**Published in
the United States**
PMB 16A
350 Fifth Ave.
Suite 3308
New York, NY
10118

**Published
in Canada**
616 Welland Ave.
St. Catharines
Ontario, Canada
L2M 5V6

**Published in the
United Kingdom**
White Cross Mills
High Town, Lancaster
LA1 4XS
United Kingdom

**Published
in Australia**
386 Mt. Alexander Rd.
Ascot Vale (Melbourne)
VIC 3032

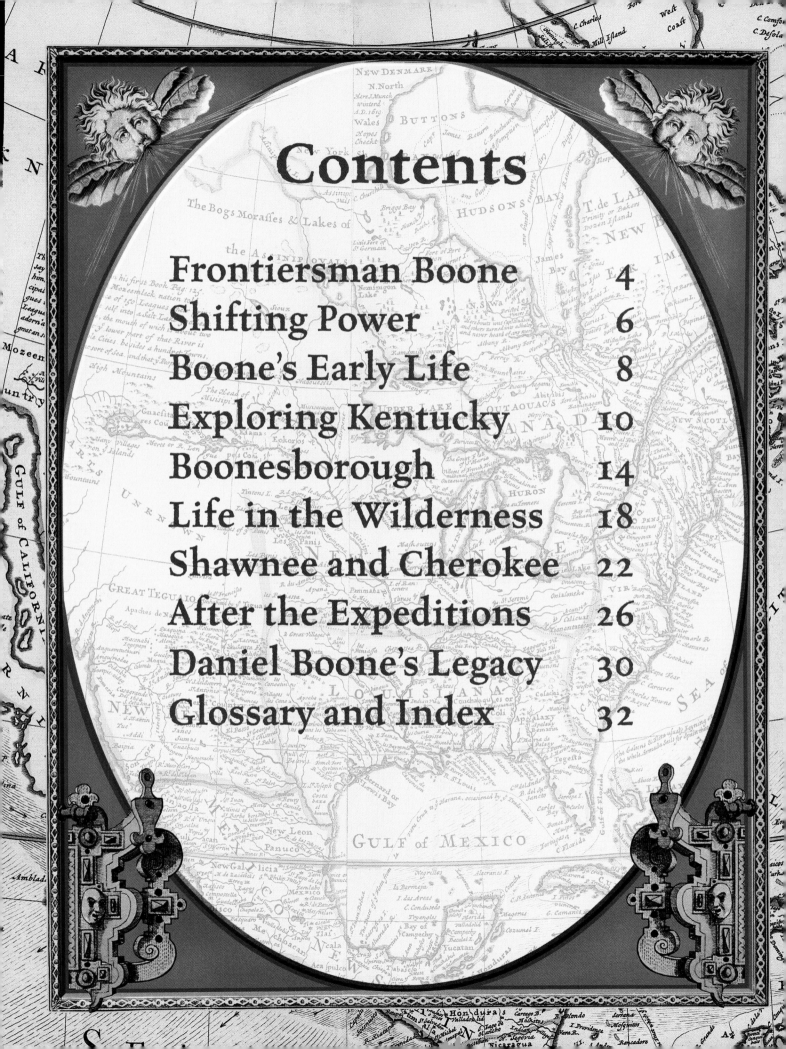

Contents

Frontiersman Boone 4

Shifting Power 6

Boone's Early Life 8

Exploring Kentucky 10

Boonesborough 14

Life in the Wilderness 18

Shawnee and Cherokee 22

After the Expeditions 26

Daniel Boone's Legacy 30

Glossary and Index 32

Frontiersman Boone

Daniel Boone was an American pioneer whose explorations led to the settlement of Kentucky. Through his travels and adventures, Boone has come to represent the American ideals of freedom and independence.

At Home in the Wilderness

Boone was known for his ability to survive in the wilderness for long periods of time, hunting deer, buffalo, and other forest animals. He loved being surrounded by nature. As an adult, Boone lived on the American frontier, the region between the wilderness and developed society. His explorations pushed the boundaries of the American frontier west of the **Appalachian Mountains** and helped open the west for settlement.

On the Trail

Boone explored as a way to acquire land and wealth for himself, and others he traveled with. During his travels, Boone both made friends with and fought with North American Native groups, including the Cherokee and Shawnee.

Daniel Boone spent a lot of his time alone in the wilderness. He even spent a whole winter living in a cave on one long hunting trip.

In the Words of...

In 1784, a book called *The Adventures of Colonel Daniel Boon* was published on Boone's 50th birthday. Written by John Filson, the book tells the story of Boone's exploration of Kentucky. Filson wrote his book as a way to attract settlers to Kentucky. While historians believe many of the book's stories are myths, the following passage shows the dangers Boone and his fellow travelers faced in the wilderness.

"In the decline of the day, near Kentucky river, as we ascended the brow of a small hill, a number of Indians rushed out upon us and made us prisoners... The Indians plundered us of what we had, and kept us in confinement seven days, treating us as common savages. During this time we expressed no desire to escape, which made them less suspicious of us... In the dead of night, as we lay by a large fire, when sleep had locked up their senses... I touched my companion, and gently awoke him. We used this favorable opportunity and departed, leaving them to take their rest, and speedily directed our course towards our old camp, but found it plundered."

Raids on both settler and Native villages were common on the frontier.

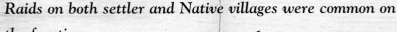

- 1713 -

Daniel's father, Squire Boone, immigrates from England to Philadelphia.

- 1734 -

Boone is born near Reading, Pennsylvania.

- 1755 -

Boone serves as part of a military expedition during the French and Indian War.

- 1756 -

Boone marries Rebecca Bryan.

Shifting Power

The British and French battled for control of North America in the years leading up to Daniel Boone's exploration of Kentucky. This struggle for power came to a head with the French and Indian War, a series of battles that took place between British and French forces from 1753 to 1760.

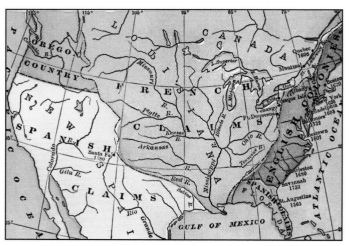

(above) At the time of the French and Indian War, there were 13 American colonies, which were controlled by the British.

(below) After the French and Indian War, also known as the Seven Years War and The Conquest in Canada, the British controlled more land in North America.

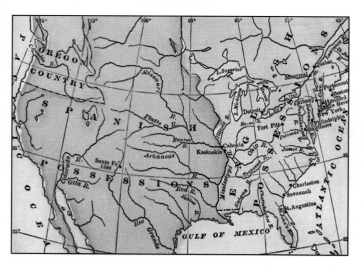

French Authority

French power in North America grew throughout the 1600s and 1700s. Before the French and Indian War, France claimed land from Canada in the north through Ohio to Louisiana in the south. French fur traders roamed the North American wilderness trapping and shooting animals, then selling the furs. Thousands of French settlers became fur traders. The French expanded their influence by establishing **alliances** with Native groups.

French and Indian War

The French and British, along with their Native allies, fought over land, forts, and **trading rights** during the French and Indian War. After winning battles at Fort Niagara, Fort Duquesne, and the Plains of Abraham, near Quebec City, the British claimed victory. The British captured Quebec City, the capital of **New France**. France lost its land in North America when the **Treaty of Paris** was signed on February 10, 1763.

Growing Anger

When the French and Indian War ended, British political leaders began trying to more tightly control American settlement, which angered many colonists. The British Proclamation of 1763 **prohibited** settlement west of the Appalachian Mountains, because Britain wanted to control trade in the area. British taxes also angered colonists. Colonists had come to North America seeking freedom from government control and wanting to own land. New British **restrictions** did not please them.

The American Revolution

The American Revolution was a series of events that ended with the 13 American **colonies** separating from the **British Empire** and the creation of the United States. One part of the revolution involved disputes over British taxation in the colonies, the other part involved the military battles of the American Revolutionary War. These battles took place from the time of the French and Indian War and ended with British defeat to colonial forces in 1783. After the American Revolution, Americans were free to push settlement farther west. Conflicts over land and **resources** in North America served as a backdrop to Daniel Boone's explorations.

(background) Colonists rebelled against the Stamp Act. The Stamp Act of 1765 required tax stamps for newspapers, playing cards, and other printed documents.

Boone's Early Life

Daniel Boone was born on November 2, 1734, in Berks County, Pennsylvania. His father, Squire Boone, was a weaver by trade, but sought to acquire land as a way to gain wealth. Daniel's mother, Sarah Morgan, ran the family farm.

Coming to America

The Boones came to North America in 1717, when George Boone, Daniel's grandfather, moved his family from England. Daniel's grandfather wanted both land and freedom to practice his Quaker religion. Quakers, also known as the Society of Friends, practiced a type of **Christianity** that was not accepted in England. Quakers did not believe in the ideals of organized Churches, such as the **Roman Catholic Church** or **Church of England**, and preached that women were equal to men in the eyes of God. Quakers were **tolerant** of other religions, including those practiced by Native Americans.

Child in the Wilderness

As a boy, Daniel Boone was easily distracted from his chores on the family farm, which included caring for his family's herd of dairy cows. Daniel often escaped to the woods, where he learned how to hunt, trap, and survive off the land. Historians are not sure if young Daniel ever attended school.

Yadkin Valley Home

In 1750, when Daniel was 15 years old, his family left Pennsylvania to settle in North Carolina's Yadkin Valley, where Squire Boone built his family a new home. By this time, Daniel had proven himself a capable hunter of deer and other animals.

Many Quakers from England settled in Pennsylvania after the colony was founded in 1681.

Boone at War

In 1755, Boone served as part of a military expedition in the French and Indian War, driving a supply wagon behind troops led by British Major General Edward Braddock. While traveling to battle the French at Fort Duquesne on the Ohio River, Braddock's forces were **ambushed** by Natives. Many were killed. Recognizing danger, Boone cut a horse free from his supply wagon and rode to safety.

Marriage

In August 1756, Boone married Rebecca Bryan. For the next ten years, he raised his family on land close to his father's home. Boone and his wife had five children during this time. During these ten years, Boone spent much of his time farming in the summer and hunting during the winter. Life changed in 1767, when Boone made an attempt to explore Kentucky. He sought a new land to hunt and possibly settle his family.

(background) Major General Edward Braddock led the British attack on French-held Fort Duquesne. Braddock was shot and died after the attack.

Exploring Kentucky

While serving in the French and Indian War, Boone met a hunter named John Findley. Findley told Boone of Kentucky, a wild and unsettled land full of deer and buffalo for hunting and a good area for farming and settlement.

NORTH AMERICA

Mississippi River

PENNSYLVANIA

Philadelphia

APPALACHIAN MOUNTAINS

KENTUCKY

Ohio River

Boonesborough

VIRGINIA

MISSOURI

Cumberland Gap Wilderness Road

NORTH CAROLINA

Yadkin Valley

TENNESSEE

Boone's Expedition through
the Cumberland Gap: →→→

Along the Warrior's Path

Boone first visited Kentucky in 1767 with his brother, Squire Boone, and a friend named William Hill. They did not find the **fertile** land that Findley had told Boone about. Two years later, Boone set out again for Kentucky, accompanied by Findley and some others. After leaving from the Yadkin River in North Carolina, the group traveled west to Powell's Valley. From Powell's Valley, a hunter's path led Boone and his group through the **Cumberland Gap** and to the Warriors' Path. The Warriors' Path was a trail through the Cumberland Gap in the Appalachian Mountains that was used by Native groups traveling to hunt buffalo. Boone's party traveled the Warriors' Path to Round Stone Lick Fort, on the western branch of the Rockcastle River in Kentucky.

(background) *After making camp, Boone climbed the highest peak on a ridge that could be seen in the distance. From the top of the ridge, Boone saw Kentucky's fertile land, full of wildlife for hunting and land for farming. Boone explored and hunted in Kentucky for two years, returning home in 1771.*

- 1767 -
Boone makes his first trip to Kentucky and hunts along the Big Sandy River.

- 1769 -
Boone is visited by John Findley before making a second trip to Kentucky.

- 1773 -
Boone leads a group of settlers to Kentucky, but is turned back by Native attack.

- 1775 -
Boone hired by the Transylvania Company to cut the Wilderness Road to Kentucky.

Settlement Effort

In 1773, Boone led a group of family members and friends in an effort to settle Kentucky, but they were turned back by a Native attack at the Cumberland Gap. Boone's son, James, was killed in the attack.

The Transylvania Company

Boone became a **trailblazer** in 1775, clearing a path to Kentucky that other settlers later followed called the Wilderness Road. Boone was hired by the Transylvania Company to build the road. The Transylvania Company wanted to own land in the west and encourage settlement. The Wilderness Road was cut on trails traditionally used by Native Americans for trade and raids by war parties, including the Warriors' Path. Boone negotiated with the Cherokee along the trail, helping secure land for the Transylvania Company.

The Wilderness Road

Boone and 30 road builders worked clearing trees and brush to create the Wilderness Road, eventually reaching Kentucky and founding a settlement. When the Wilderness Road was completed, it was 300 miles (483 kilometers) long, extending from Pennsylvania, eastern Virginia, and North Carolina through the Cumberland Gap and into Kentucky. The Wilderness Road made it possible for settlers to reach Kentucky.

(background) Loaded with provisions, Boone attempts to re-settle his family in Kentucky. Boone's son, James, was killed in an attack by Native Americans during the journey. After James' death, the Boone family returned to North Carolina.

Boonesborough

In the spring of 1775, Boone and the Wilderness Road builders established a settlement on the Kentucky River near Otter Creek.

Boone's Settlement

The settlers constructed what was first called Fort Boone, made up of four to six log cabins on the south side of the Kentucky River. Richard Henderson, a shareholder in the Transylvania Company, eventually changed the name to Boonesborough and drew up plans for an expanded settlement. To attract people to the area, the Transylvania Company offered settlers free land if they planted crops. The more settlers who moved into Kentucky, the more the value of the land increased. The Transylvania Company would make more money selling land if this happened. Eighty men made their way to Boonesborough in the settlement's early days.

New Government

Shortly after the settlement of Boonesborough, Henderson arranged a meeting with the settlers of Kentucky to form a government. A government would officially allow the Transylvania Company to own and distribute land to settlers. Daniel Boone was elected as a government representative of the new colony called Transylvania, which included Kentucky. Enough settlers came to Kentucky that it was made a county of Virginia in 1776.

(background) Fort Boone took nearly three years to complete. It was built to defend settlers against Native attack.

Hard Living

Settlers at Boonesborough worked hard clearing land and cutting down trees. Wood from the trees was used to construct buildings. Crops were planted near the settlement for food. Early Kentucky settlers lived under hard conditions in the wilderness. Despite an abundance of wildlife, too much hunting near Boonesborough quickly took its toll. Settlers had to travel farther from the settlement to hunt buffalo, deer, and other animals. Adding to this problem was that too few crops were planted, leading to a food shortage. Supplies were eventually brought in using the Wilderness Road. The construction of Boonesborough continued in the face of these problems and was completed in 1778.

In July 1776, Boone's daughter, Jemima, and two of her friends, were captured by a group of Cherokee and Shawnees. Boone and some settlers set out after the group, eventually overtaking them, storming the Native camp, and rescuing the girls.

Uneasy Relations

Relations with Native groups around Boonesborough were not peaceful. A settler was killed in an attack the fourth day after Boone's arrival. In February 1778, Boone set out alone to hunt and was ambushed by Natives and taken prisoner. Boone was taken to a camp where 300 Shawnee warriors led by a chief named Blackfish were preparing to attack Boonesborough. Boone told Blackfish he would convince some Boonesborough settlers to surrender if Boonesborough was spared.

Prisoners of the Shawnee

Twenty-six men surrendered and were soon after taken prisoner by the Shawnee. Boone convinced Blackfish to spare the prisoners' lives. While a prisoner at the Native camp, Boone learned that Native forces were still gathering to attack Boonesborough. He needed to warn the settlers. While the Shawnee men were distracted hunting turkeys one day, Boone escaped. Upon his return to Boonesborough, Boone directed the settlers to begin reinforcing, or strengthening, the fort.

The Attack on Boonesborough

A **war party** of more than 440 Native warriors led by Blackfish approached Boonesborough. The British supplied guns and commanded the Native attack in an attempt to exert control of colonials in the area. Upon reaching the settlement, Blackfish demanded that Boone and the people of Boonesborough surrender. Two days of **negotiations** failed and fighting broke out. Boone and the settlers at Boonesborough withstood two days of constant fire and began to wait out the Natives, who in the following days tried to burn down the settlement, and even dig a tunnel into it. All Native efforts to take Boonesborough were turned back. Blackfish and his men began their **retreat**. About thirty-seven Natives died in fighting, compared to two Boonesborough settlers.

Boonesborough was attacked by the Shawnee in 1777 and in 1778. Other new settlements in Kentucky, such as Harrodsburg, were also attacked.

- 1775 -
Boonesborough settlement is established.

- 1776 -
Kentucky is made a county of Virginia.

- 1778 -
Attack on Boonesborough.

Life in the Wilderness

On Boone's early journeys, he took only what was needed. His supplies included guns, traps, ammunition, and blankets.

Survival

Frontier explorers carried **long rifles** for hunting and protection. They also carried hunting knives. Their clothing was often made from animal skins. Many explorers and settlers, including Boone, wore hats made of beaver fur. While exploring Kentucky, Boone had little problem finding food to eat. The wilderness held a great amount of wildlife, including buffalo and turkey.

Attracting Game

Food was often cooked over an open fire. Gathering salt at salt licks was an important part of life in the wilderness. Salt licks are areas where natural deposits of salt form and attract animals seeking nutrients that salt provides. Salt licks were good areas for hunting, as well as for gathering salt for cooking and **preserving** meat.

Daniel Boone used a type of gun called a long rifle. These guns were called long rifles because the barrels were as long as four feet (one meter).

Boone and other hunters marked trails, sometimes carving into trees to remember the path they had traveled.

Beef Jerky

During his travels, Boone ate dried meat, known as jerky, to survive in the wilderness. Ask an adult to help you make beef jerky.

Ingredients:

3 lbs beef (1.4 kg)

2/3 cup (160 ml) Worcestershire sauce

2/3 cup (160 ml) soy sauce

1 tsp (5 ml) black pepper

1 tsp (5 ml) garlic powder

1 tsp (5 ml) onion powder

Directions:

1. Cut meat into thin slices.

2. Mix all other ingredients in a large plastic zipper bag.

3. Add sliced meat to bag and refrigerate. Turn bag to mix meat every two hours. Refrigerate overnight.

4. Drain meat in a colander and pat dry with paper towels.

5. Place a sheet of aluminum foil on bottom rack of oven. Set oven at lowest temperature.

6. Carefully place meat slices directly onto foil. Leave the oven door open a crack to allow moisture to escape.

Drying time takes between four and 12 hours, depending on the thickness of meat slices. The best beef jerky is firm and dry, not spongy.

(background) Boone was often away for long periods of time on hunting trips. Hunters set up camp and used it as a base while they were out hunting animals for their furs. The animal furs were brought to town at the end of the season and sold.

Winter Hunts

Boone and his traveling companions were at the mercy of the weather. While many of Boone's travels took place during summer months, the best hunting was often done in the winter. Hunters wore animal skins and furs during winter months, which protected them from cold temperatures. Warmth was also generated by campfire.

Natural Remedies

Illness and injury were not uncommon for Boone. Cuts and other injuries were often suffered during his wilderness travel and hunting trips. Boone used **natural remedies** to heal some of these cuts, including an **ointment** made with oak bark peeled from a tree and pounded into a jam-like substance. Boone learned of natural remedies from Native groups and hunters when he was young.

Daniel Boone's skills as a hunter are legendary. In this illustration, an artist shows Boone wrestling a bear. Although this event may not have happened, Boone did hunt bear for its meat.

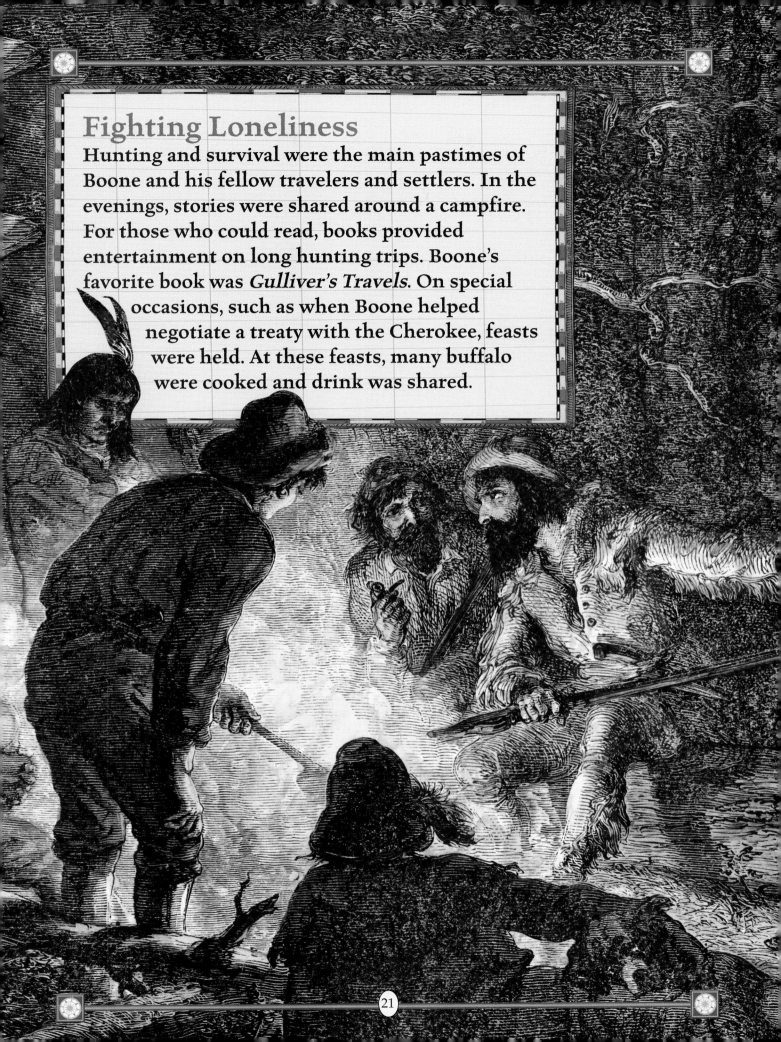

Fighting Loneliness

Hunting and survival were the main pastimes of Boone and his fellow travelers and settlers. In the evenings, stories were shared around a campfire. For those who could read, books provided entertainment on long hunting trips. Boone's favorite book was *Gulliver's Travels*. On special occasions, such as when Boone helped negotiate a treaty with the Cherokee, feasts were held. At these feasts, many buffalo were cooked and drink was shared.

Shawnee and Cherokee

Before European settlement, more than 30 Native tribes lived in the northeast area of North America. These tribes belonged to one of two major language groups, the Algonquian or Iroquoian. These groups spoke different languages and had different customs and traditions.

Warring Nations

Relations between some Algonquian and Iroquoian groups were not peaceful. They fought over territory and alliances with Europeans and Americans. Daniel Boone came into contact with several Native tribes, including the Shawnee and Cherokee. The Shawnee spoke an Algonquian language and the Cherokee an Iroquoian language.

Natural Life

North American Native peoples relied on their natural environment for survival, hunting, and farming for food. Men were responsible for hunting animals such as deer using bow and arrows. Meat from the animals was eaten and their skins were used to make shelter and clothing. Bones of animals were used to make tools, including cooking utensils. Native men also cleared land suitable for planting. Women planted and cared for crops including corn, pumpkin, beets, squash, and tomatoes.

(background) Corn was a major Native American crop. Food was also found in the forest, where berries, apples, and nuts were harvested. Natives peoples ate fish caught in rivers and streams, which they traveled using canoes.

Native and Frontier Women

Natives and frontier settlers shared common ways of life. The lives of women on the frontier and Native women were in some ways similar, as husbands often left for long periods of time on hunting trips. Both Native and frontier women took care of the crops and raised the children.

With their husbands away, frontier women also had to defend the home against intruders.

Native Leaders

Chiefs were the leaders of Native communities. Groups could have more than one chief, each with a different area of responsibility.

Certain chiefs oversaw war while others ensured village life ran smoothly. There was a common belief among Native groups in a "great spirit," which gave life to all things. Animals and plants found in nature were important **spiritual** symbols for Native groups. Spiritual leaders in Native communities helped heal the sick and injured, both physically and spiritually. Natural remedies found in the forests were used for different healing purposes by Native tribes.

The Cherokee crafted masks out of wood or gourds called Booger masks. The masks were thought to represent evil spirits and were worn in ceremonies.

Adopted Family

When Boone was taken prisoner by the Shawnee, he did not resist his captivity. He was familiar and friendly with the natives, even going on hunting trips with men in the tribe. It was a Native tradition that some prisoners of war were adopted to replace dead family members. Boone became well liked by Blackfish, the chief who adopted him, and was given the native name "shel-tow-ee" or "big turtle."

(above) Look closely for the Native hunters in this illustration of a traditional hunting method. After the arrival of Europeans, Native groups began using guns for hunting. Competition for hunting grounds increased among Native groups and settlers, as the supply of animals decreased.

Friends and Enemies

In Boone's many encounters with the Shawnee and Cherokee, he made friends and enemies among both. In 1775, Boone traveled to friendly Cherokee villages around Kentucky, trying to convince the Cherokee to attend a peace treaty meeting being held at Sycamore Shoals, Tennessee. The meeting took place on March 17, 1775, and a treaty was signed. For three wagon loads of goods such as clothing, blankets, firearms, alcohol, and other items, the Cherokee gave the Transylvania Company the right to settle Kentucky.

(below) Some Algonquin speaking Native groups made dome-shaped wigwams. After contact with settlers, some Native villages were modeled after frontier settlements, with log cabins mixed among wigwams.

After the Expeditions

In 1779, Daniel Boone decided to leave Boonesborough and explore new opportunities, first founding a village in Kentucky called Boone's Station. In the years after, he led attacks against Shawnee villages, hunted, worked as a land surveyor, and moved his family a number of times.

Active Life

In 1781, Boone was elected as a representative in the **Virginia Assembly**. Two years later, he moved his family to Limestone, on the Ohio River, opened a tavern, and worked surveying land along the Ohio River. In 1784, *The Adventures of Colonel Daniel Boon*, by John Filson, was published. The book was written to encourage people to settle in Kentucky, telling of the area's fertile land and good hunting.

On the Move

As years passed, more American settlers moved west into Kentucky. The area was becoming too populated and regulated by government for Boone's liking. Despite his role in settling Kentucky, Boone eventually lost all of his property there because the United States government did not recognize his land claim.

An advertising poster from the 1830s. Before railroads were built, trails and roads were the only way of travel overland. Land surveyors were hired by companies building roads to map the areas and determine the best route for the roads to pass through.

Land in Missouri

In 1797, Boone's son, Daniel Morgan Boone, traveled to Missouri to **scout** land. The Spanish controlled Missouri and other territories in the west of North America, and Spanish authorities invited the Boones to **immigrate**. In 1798, Boone led his family west to Missouri. He was appointed leader of a district in Missouri and granted land there. After settling in Missouri, Boone made two more trips to Kentucky before his death.

The Louisiana Purchase

With the 1803 Louisiana Purchase, the United States bought more than 800,000 square miles (two million square kilometers) of land from France for 15 million dollars. The land stretched from New Orleans, Louisiana, in the south to Canada in the north. It also included Missouri. Following the Louisiana Purchase, Boone went to the United States government asking for recognition of his land ownership in Missouri, which he did not get until 1814.

President Thomas Jefferson originally only wanted to buy the French port of New Orleans from the French. French foreign minister Talleyrand instead offered to sell all of the Louisiana territory to the United States. The purchase more than doubled the size of the country.

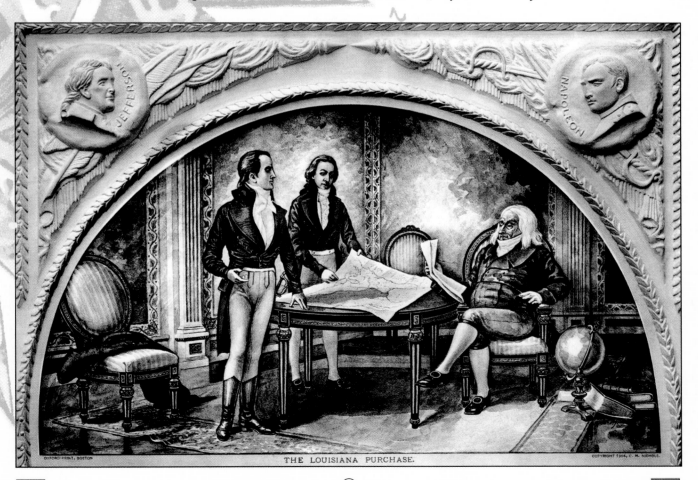

THE LOUISIANA PURCHASE.

Boone's Death

Daniel Boone died on September 26, 1820, three days after falling ill and refusing medication from the doctor. He was 85 years old. He was buried on family land next to his wife, who had died in 1813. Boone's explorations had directly led to the settlement of Kentucky, but he contributed more to the foundations of America. By 1800, more than 200,000 settlers had used the Wilderness Road to settle in the area. Commerce, trade, and businesses grew after people populated areas of Kentucky Boone had explored.

Changing Ways

As American settlers pushed into Kentucky and farther west, Native American groups such as the Shawnee and Cherokee were forced off their traditional lands. Native Americans could do little to stop the settlers from coming. Some Native groups eventually relocated farther west, others joined together. With fewer and fewer animals available to hunt, the lifestyle of Native groups changed. By the 1860s, Native Americans were forced onto Reservations, or certain areas of land set aside by the Federal Government for them. Reservations were only a small fraction of the land Native peoples held before American settlers moved past the Appalachians and into the West.

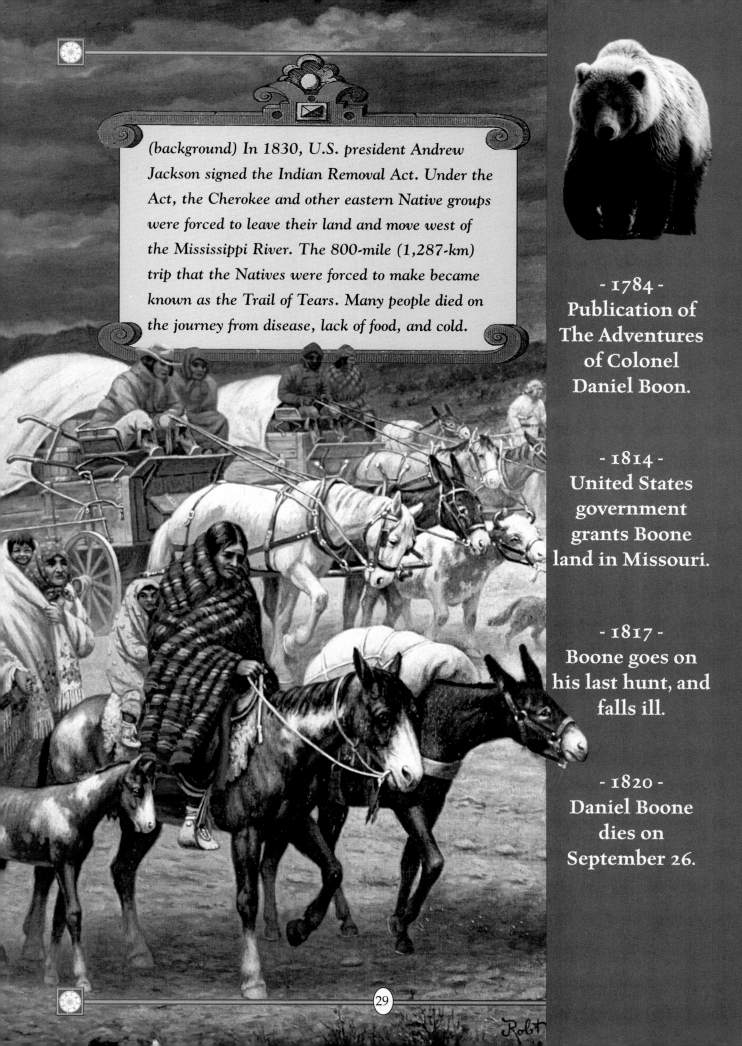

(background) In 1830, U.S. president Andrew Jackson signed the Indian Removal Act. Under the Act, the Cherokee and other eastern Native groups were forced to leave their land and move west of the Mississippi River. The 800-mile (1,287-km) trip that the Natives were forced to make became known as the Trail of Tears. Many people died on the journey from disease, lack of food, and cold.

- 1784 -
Publication of The Adventures of Colonel Daniel Boon.

- 1814 -
United States government grants Boone land in Missouri.

- 1817 -
Boone goes on his last hunt, and falls ill.

- 1820 -
Daniel Boone dies on September 26.

Daniel Boone's Legacy

Daniel Boone's travels helped open the west for early American settlers who followed in his footsteps. Boone is remembered for his feats as a frontiersman, able to survive in the wilderness while exploring, blazing trails, and building forts.

Remembering Boone

Many sites in America pay tribute to Daniel Boone. The Boone Homestead near Reading, Pennsylvania, where Daniel Boone was born, is today a museum open to the public. The famous Wilderness Road that Daniel Boone helped create is today part of U.S. Route 25, or the Dixie Highway, one of the most historic in America. Part of the wilderness Boone traveled and explored is today a 704,000 acre (284,909 hectare) forest in eastern Kentucky, known as the Daniel Boone National Forest. Even the site of Boone's death in Charles County, Missouri, is today a museum.

Inspiring Exploration

Members of the Boone family continued moving west after Daniel Boone's death. His son, Daniel Morgan Boone, was one of the first settlers of Kansas. Boone's grandson explored the Rocky Mountains.

A statue stands at the Museum of the Cherokee Indian in North Carolina.

Famous American explorers Meriwether Lewis (top) and William Clark (bottom) expanded upon Boone's exploration of the West when they set out from Missouri to reach the Pacific Ocean on the Oregon coast.

American Legend

After the publication of *The Adventures of Colonel Daniel Boon*, Boone became a role model for other pioneers who settled the west of North America. Over time, Boone became an American legend, with many myths surrounding his life and adventures. Hundreds of books, television programs, movies, and stories tell of Boone's life and adventures. Many of them are not based on fact and have added to myths surrounding him.

(background) Actors portray Daniel Boone and his brother, Israel, in a 1960s TV series.

Glossary

alliance A partnership between peoples or countries

ambush To hide and wait for an enemy to approach before attacking by surprise

Appalachian Mountains A mountain chain in eastern North America extending from Newfoundland, Canada, to the U.S. state of Alabama

British Empire The areas around the world colonized by England starting in the 1600s

Christianity A religion based on the teachings of Jesus Christ, whom Christians believe is the son of God

Church of England A Christian religion founded in 1534 with the ruler of England at its head. Also called the Anglican Church

colonies Areas of land ruled by a distant country

Cumberland Gap A natural pass through the Cumberland Plateau, or Cumberland Mountains, in the Appalachians

fertile Able to produce abundant crops or vegetation

immigrate To move from one place to another

long rifle A type of rifle used in early America that had a long barrel

natural remedies Medicines made from substances found in nature, such as plants and tree bark

negotiation A discussion between two or more sides in order to reach an agreement

New France France's colonies in North America

ointment A salve used on the skin for healing

preserve To keep food from rotting

prohibited Something that is illegal

resources Things found in nature that are used by people, such as furs, water, and minerals

restrictions Laws or decrees that control or place limitations on someone or something

retreat To withdraw from a fight

Roman Catholic Church A branch of Christianity that focuses on traditional religious beliefs, practices, and rituals. The head of the Roman Catholic Church is the Pope, in Rome

scout Someone who finds information

spiritual Relating to the soul of a person or animal, or to gods and supernatural beings

tolerant Willingness to accept or understand

trading rights Permission granted to trade in certain goods or areas

trailblazer Someone who cuts a path or trail

Treaty of Paris An agreement signed between France and England in 1763 in which France gave up its rights to New France

tribe A group that shares common ancestry, culture, and leaders

Virginia Assembly The first legislature in the U.S.

war party A band of warriors

Index

Adventures of Colonel Daniel Boon, The 5, 26, 29, 31
American Revolution 7
Appalachian Mountains 4, 7, 28

beaver fur hats 18
beef jerky recipe 19
Blackfish 16-17, 24
Boone family 5, 8, 9, 10, 12, 13, 16, 26, 27, 28, 30, 31
Boone historical sites 30
Boone legends 20, 31
Boonesborough 14-17, 26
Boone's Station 26
British 6-7
British taxation 7

Cherokee 4, 12, 16, 21, 22, 24, 25, 28, 29, 30

Cumberland Gap 10, 12

Findley, John 10, 11
Fort Boone 14
French 5, 6, 7, 9, 27
French and Indian War 5, 6, 7, 9, 10
frontier women 23
fur traders 6, 19

General Edward Braddock 9

hunting 4, 8, 9, 10, 11, 15, 16, 18-21, 22, 23, 24, 25, 26, 29, 30

Kentucky 4, 9, 10-13, 14-17, 18, 25, 26, 27, 28, 30

land surveyors 26
long rifle 18
Louisiana Purchase 27

Missouri 27, 29, 31

Native Americans 4, 5, 6, 9, 10, 11, 12, 13, 14, 16-17, 20, 22-25, 28, 29, 30
Native American women 22-23
North Carolina 8, 10, 12, 13, 30

peace treaty 21, 25
Pennsylvania 5, 8, 12

Quakers 8

settlers 4, 5, 6, 7, 11, 12, 13, 14-17, 18, 21, 22, 26, 28, 30

Shawnee 4, 16, 17, 22, 24, 25, 26, 28
Spanish 27
Sycamore Shoals 25

trailblazer 12
Trail of Tears 29
Transylvania Company 11, 12, 14, 25

Virginia Assembly 26

Warriors' Path 10, 12
wigwams 25
Wilderness Road 11, 12, 14, 15, 28, 30

1 2 3 4 5 6 7 8 9 0 Printed in the U.S.A. 5 4 3 2 1 0 9 8 7 6